Bon

A dictionary of French restaurant terms

Understand what's on the menu and know
what you are ordering

Concorde French Language Publications

Publishers of books and magazines for learners of French

8, Skye Close, Maidstone ME15 9SJ, United Kingdom

www.concordefrench.com

10-digit ISBN: 0-9545991-2-8
13-digit ISBN: 978-0-9545991-2-68

INTRODUCTION

France has a long history of culinary excellence, largely shaped by its geography: vast fertile areas, mountains, long coastlines, salt marshes … There are thus strong regional variations in its rich cuisine, made even more varied by influences from the many adjoining countries.

Consequently when dining out, you can look forward to great choice. But this choice can result in menus being quite daunting as these regional influences are often reflected in the names and descriptions of the dishes. Even the French will often ask the waiter for an explanation of what is included in a particular dish.

This pocket guide aims to help you navigate your way through the menu to the successful ordering of a satisfying meal. However, for the reasons given above, it is impossible to have a totally comprehensive guide to menu terms. We have therefore tried to concentrate on those that will be most often encountered. We hope we have succeeded and that you find our guide useful.

Bon appétit!

Margaret & Kenneth Murray
Concorde French Language Publications

Abricot	Apricot
Agneau de lait	Milk-fed lamb, yearling. **~ de pré-salé** - lamb raised on salt marshes
Agrumes	Citrus fruit
Aiglefin (or **Aigrefin)**	Haddock
Aigre-doux	Sweet-and-sour
Aigrette	Cheese fritter
Ail	Garlic
Aïoli (or **Ailloli)**	Garlic mayonnaise, usually made with olive oil
Airelle	Bilberry, huckleberry or wortleberry
Algues	Seaweed
Allumettes	Matchstick-shaped. **Pommes ~** - thin-cut fried potatoes
Alouette	Lark, often prepared as a pâté
Aloyau	Sirloin or tenderloin of beef
Alsacienne, à 1'	Alsace-style: with sauerkraut, sausage, potatoes and sometimes foie gras. Can also refer to chicken or fish cooked in Riesling
Amande	Almond
Amande de mer	Small clam-like shellfish
Amandine	Almond-flavoured
Américaine, à 1'	See Armoricaine
Amuse-bouche (or **Amuse-gueule)**	Appetiser or cocktail snack
Ananas	Pineapple
Anchoïade	Paste made of anchovies and garlic, usually eaten on toast
Anchois	Anchovy
Ancienne, à l'	In the old style: first braised then simmered as in a blanquette or a fricassée
Andouille	Large sausage made from chitterlings

	(tripe). Usually eaten cold
Andouillette	Small chitterling (tripe) sausage. Usually fried or grilled
Aneth	Dill
Anglaise, à l'	Coated with breadcrumbs and fried
Anguille	Eel
Anguille de mer	Conger eel
Anis	Aniseed
Araignée de mer	Spider crab
Armoricaine	Breton-style (Armorique = Brittany) sauce (white wine, cognac, tomatoes and butter)
Aromate	Spice
Artichaut	Globe artichoke. ***Fond d'*** ~ - bottom; ***coeur d'*** ~ - heart; ~ ***à la barigoule***- stuffed with ham, mushrooms, onions, etc.
Asperge	Asparagus. ***Pointe d'*** ~ - asparagus tip
Assaisonné(e) de (or **avec**)	Seasoned with
Assiette (de)	Plate (of)
Assiette anglaise	Assorted cold meats
Assiette campagnarde	Assorted local cold meat produce
Assortiment	Variety, assortment
Aumônière	A dish in which the ingredients are rolled into a purse-shaped pastry
Autruche	Ostrich
Avocat	Avocado (pear)

Baba au rhum	Rum baba. Sponge cake soaked in rum
Baie	Berry
Ballotine	Any meat, poultry or fish that has been boned and rolled. Served hot or cold, and sometimes stuffed
Bambou	Bamboo. **Pousse de** ~ - bamboo shoots
Banane	Banana. ~ **au four** - baked banana ~ **flambée** - with vanilla and rum and flambéed
Bar	Bass or sea perch
Baron d'agneau	Lamb joint comprising the saddle and both hind legs
Barquette	Boat-shaped pastry shell, variously filled
Basilic	Basil
Basquaise	With tomatoes and peppers, and often rice and Bayonne ham, as in **poulet basquaise**
Bavarois	Bavarian cream. Cold dessert containing whipped cream and egg-custard, often served with fruit
Bavette	Cut of beef equivalent to skirt or flank
Bécasse	Woodcock
Bécassine	Snipe
Béchamel	Sauce made with flour, butter and milk
Beignet	Small sweet or savoury fritter
Belle-Hélène	See **Poire**
Belon	Oyster (see **Huîtres**)
Bette	Swiss chard
Betterave rouge	Beetroot
Beurre blanc	Sauce with butter, shallots, wine vinegar and sometimes white wine

Beurre d'anchois	Anchovy butter
Beurre maître d'hôtel	Butter with parsley, lemon-juice, salt and pepper
Biche	Female deer
Bifteck	Steak
Bifteck haché	Hamburger
Bigorneau	Winkle
Biscuit	Biscuit, cookie. A light, dry sponge-cake such as **biscuit de Savoie**
Biscuit à la cuiller	Sponge finger
Bisque	Thick soup, usually of shellfish or of game
Blanc (de volaille, de poulet)	White breast (of chicken). Can also describe white fish fillet (e.g. *blanc de turbot*)
Blanquette	Stew made of veal, lamb, chicken or seafood, served in a creamy sauce with onions and mushrooms
Blinis	Small, thick pancakes from Russia, traditionally eaten with caviar
Bœuf à la mode	Beef braised in red wine with vegetables and herbs served either cold in jelly or hot
Bœuf bourguignon	Beef cooked in red wine with mushrooms, onions and bacon
Bœuf en daube	Beef stewed in red wine with bacon, salt pork and vegetables
Bœuf Stroganoff	Beef strips, sour cream, onions, mushrooms
Bombe glacée	Ice cream dessert consisting of two ice-creams (or water-ice) mixtures such as **Bombe dame-blanche** – vanilla outside, almond within
Bonne-femme	White wine sauce, shallots, mushrooms, usually served with sole or poultry
Bordelaise, à la	Bordeaux-style: with a red wine sauce made of garlic or shallots and parsley

6

Bortsch	Beetroot soup with sour cream, of Russian origin
Bouchée à la Reine	Little puff-pastry (**vol-au-vent**) cases filled with chicken and mushrooms in a cream sauce
Boudin	Large sausage or meat pudding. ~ **blanc** - white pudding made from white meat, eggs and cream and sometimes truffles, traditionally served at Christmas; ~ **noir** - black pudding made with pig's blood
Bouillabaisse	Mediterranean fish stew or soup made from a variety of fish, olive oil, garlic, tomatoes and saffran
Bouillon	Stock, broth, soup
Boulette	Small ball of fish or minced meat, dipped in batter and fried, or baked
Bouquet	Prawn
Bourdaloue	Whole fruit in a pastry case
Brandade de morue	Salt cod pounded to a cream with milk, garlic and olive oil
Brillat-Savarin	Famous gourmet (1755-1826) whose name is given to a number of dishes, often including foie gras and truffles
Brioche	Bun or small cake made from a rich dough incorporating butter and eggs
Broche, à la	Spit roasted
Brochet	Fresh-water pike
Brochette	Meat or fish on a skewer
Brugnon	Nectarine
Bûche de Noël	A Christmas log, made of a rolled sponge-cake, usually filled with chestnut and chocolate
Bûche glacée	Ice cream in the shape of a log, served at Christmas

Cabillaud	Fresh cod
Cabri	Kid, young goat
Caen, à la mode de	Cooked in Calvados and white wine
Caille	Quail
Cajou, noix d'	Cashew nut
Cake	Fruit-cake
Calamar (or **Calmar**)	Squid
Campagne, de	Country style, rustic. **Pâté de campagne** - rough-cut pâté often containing mushrooms
Canapé	Little round of bread spread with a tasty filling eaten as a cocktail snack
Canard	Duck
Caneton	Duckling
Cannelle	Cinnamon
Câpres	Capers
Carbonnade de bœuf	Braised beef in beer and onions, from the North and East of France
Cari	Curry
Carottes râpées	Grated carrots
Carpaccio	Very thin slices of raw, cured beef served with condiments
Carpe	Carp, freshwater fish
Carré d'agneau	Lamb chops. Rack or loin of lamb
Carré de porc	Pork cutlets
Carré de veau	Veal chops; best end of neck cutlets
Carrelet	Flounder, plaice
Cassate	A 'two-tone' ice-cream with Chantilly cream and crystallized fruit
Cassis	Blackcurrant
Cassolette	Individual cooking dish, used for various fruit or cream desserts, or starters

Cassonade	Soft brown sugar, demerara sugar
Cassoulet	Stew from the Languedoc region based on white haricot beans, sausage and pork. The Toulouse version includes goose, and the Carcassonne version, lamb.
Céleri (en branche)	Celery (stalks)
Céleri-rave	Celeriac
Cendres, sous les	Cooked (buried) in hot ashes
Cèpe (also known as **bolet**)	Fine, delicate mushrooms often used in omelettes
Cerf	Stag, deer, red deer, venison
Cerfeuil	Chervil
Cerise (noire)	(Black) cherry
Cervelas	Saveloy, pork garlic sausage, served hot or cold as an hors d'oeuvre
Cervelle	Brains, usually calf's or lamb's
Chair à saucisse	Sausage meat
Champenoise, à la	In the Champagne-style, as in **potée à la champenoise** - Stew of ham, bacon and sausage, with cabbage
Champignons	Mushrooms
Chanterelle	Apricot-coloured mushroom, also known as **girolle**
Chantilly	With whipped cream
Chapelure	Breadcrumbs
Chapon	Capon. A castrated cock
Charbon de bois, au	Grilled on charcoal
Charcuterie (assortie)	(A variety of) cold pork cuts, such as **saucisson**, **saucisse**, ham
Charentais, melon	Variety of sweet melon
Charlotte	Hot pudding with fruit (usually apples) inside a bread/sponge lined mould. Also, ~ **russe** - sponge-fingers lining with a cream, mousse or fruit filling, served cold

9

Chasseur	Hunter's style. Garnished with a sauce made with mushrooms, shallots and parsley
Châtaigne	Sweet chestnut, also known as **marron**
Chateaubriand	Thick fillet steak, porterhouse steak
Chaud-froid	Cooked game or game fowl served cold in white sauce and aspic. ~ **de volaille** - a cold, jellied poultry dish
Chausson	A puff pastry turnover, often containing fruit
Chemise, en	Describes any dish or ingredient which is coated or wrapped in a pastry, vine leaves, etc.
Cheval	Horsemeat
Chèvre	Goat. Goat's cheese
Chevreau	Kid, young goat
Chevreuil	Roedeer, roe-buck. Also venison
Chich	Kebab
Chicon	Chicory
Chicorée frisée	Curly endive
Chiffonnade	Thinly-cut leaves of lettuce or sorrel
Chinoise, à la	Chinese-style: with bean sprouts and soy sauce
Chipirone	Squid
Chips	Potato crisps
Chocolat au lait	Milk chocolate
Choix, au	A choice of. E.g. **une omelette au choix** – the customer can choose the filling
Chorizo	Very spicy sausage – originating from Spain and found in the Pyrenean provinces
Chou(x)	Cabbage. ~ **farci** - stuffed cabbage; ~ **fleur** - cauliflower; ~ **rave** - kohlrabi; ~ **rouge** - red cabbage; ~ **de Bruxelles** - Brussels sprouts
Choux, pâte à	Choux pastry: dough made with

	flour, water, butter and eggs. Used for éclairs and profiteroles
Chou à la crème	Éclair, cream bun
Chou au fromage	Cheese puff
Choucroute garnie	Sauerkraut with pork, sausages, bacon, boiled ham and/or goose meat and potatoes
Ciboulette	Chives
Citron	Lemon. ~ **vert** - lime
Citrouille	Pumpkin. Also called **potiron**
Civet	Rich stew or ragoût, usually of hare or venison, with mushrooms, onions and bacon in red wine, and thickened with blood
Civet de lièvre	Jugged hare
Clafoutis	A pudding made with fruit (usually cherries) baked in a batter
Claire	Type of oyster (see **Huîtres**)
Clou de girofle	Clove (spice)
Cochon de lait	Suckling pig
Cochonnaille (*fam.*)	See **Charcuterie**

Cocotte, en	Cooked in a casserole dish
Cœur de	Heart of an animal or the centre of various vegetables (e.g. artichokes)
Cœur de palmier	Tender shoots of the palm tree, palm heart, served with a vinaigrette as an hors d'oeuvre
Coing	Quince

Colin	Hake, also called **saumon blanc**
Collet (or **collier**)	Scrag of mutton, neck of mutton
Compote	Stewed fruit, usually served cold
Concombre	Cucumber
Condé	Poached fruit (apricots or pears) in syrup served hot on rice
Confit de canard, de dinde, d'oie, de porc	Duck, turkey, goose or pork cooked and preserved in its own fat
Confit(e)	Preserved or candied
Confiture	Jam. ~ **d'oranges** - marmalade
Congre	Conger eel
Consommé	Clear soup
Contrefilet (or **faux-filet**)	Sirloin, usually tied for roasting
Coq (au vin)	Chicken. (Chicken in red wine sauce with mushrooms, onions and herbs)
Coque	Cockle
Coque, oeuf à la	Soft-boiled served in a *coquetier* (egg cup)
Coquillages	Shellfish in general
Coquille	Shell-shaped bowl in which dishes are served (i.e. fish in a creamy sauce)
Coquille St-Jacques	Scallop. **Corail de** ~ - pink part of the scallop
Corbeille (**de fruits, de pain**)	Basket (of fruit, of bread)
Coriandre	Coriander
Cornet	Conical pastry filled with cream. Ice-cream cone. Also a side of ham rolled in a cone shape and filled with some filling
Cornichon	Gherkin
Côte d'agneau	Lamb chop
Côte de bœuf	Side of beef
Côte de veau	Veal chop
Côtelette	Chop

Cotriade	White fish and shellfish stew, with potatoes and onions. A speciality of Brittany
Cou	Neck of animal or fowl
Cou d'oie farci	Goose neck stuffed with foie gras, minced pork and truffles, served cold in slices
Couenne	Pork rind, crackling, a speciality of Périgord
Coulibiac de saumon or ~ **de volaille**	Salmon or chicken tourte served as a hot entrée, Russian in origin
Coulis (de)	Thick sauce or purée (of)
Coupe glacée	Sundae, ice-cream dessert
Courge	Pumpkin
Courgette	Courgette, baby marrow
Couronne	Circle or ring *(une couronne – a crown)*
Couronne de côtelettes rôties	Crown roast of lamb
Court-bouillon	Aromatic poaching liquid. Broth based on vegetable stock
Couscous	Semolina. North-African dish with lamb, chicken and vegetables in a spicy **harissa** sauce and served with semolina couscous
Crabe à l'anglaise	Dressed crab
Cramique	Flemish raisin or currant loaf
Crème, à la	Served with cream or cooked in cream sauce. ~ **anglaise** - light custard sauce; ~ **brûlée** - rich cream custard with a topping of burnt brown sugar; ~ **caramel** or **crème renversée** or **flan** - vanilla custard with caramel sauce; ~ **Chantilly** - whipped cream containing sugar and vanilla; ~ **fouettée** - whipped cream; ~ **fraîche** - lightly soured cream; ~ **frangipane** - a type of

13

vanilla pastry cream; ~ **Mont-Blanc** - chestnut and cream purée; ~ **pâtissière** - custard made with eggs, sugar, flour, milk and vanilla

Créole, à la — Creole style: with rice, sweet peppers and tomatoes. Also desserts and puddings with rice

Crêpe (dentelle) — Thin pancake. ~ **fourrée** - stuffed pancake; ~ **Suzette** - sweet pancake with orange liqueur sauce

Crépinette de — Wrapping of

Cresson — Watercress

Crevette grise — Shrimp

Crevette rose — Prawn

Croque Monsieur — Toasted cheese and ham sandwich

Croque Madame — Toasted cheese and ham sandwich with a fried egg on top

Croquette — Food (potatoes, fish) shaped into oval or cylinder forms, covered in egg and breadcrumbs and deep-fried. **Pommes** ~ - creamed potatoes, breadcrumbed and fried

Croustade — Small pastry mould with various fillings

Croûte, en — Cooked inside a pastry case

Croûtons — Small cubes of crisp bread fired or toasted and used to garnish salads or soups

Cru(e) — Raw

Crudités — Selection of raw vegetables served as a starter

Crustacés — Shellfish, seafood

Cuisse — Thigh, leg. ~ **s de grenouille** - frog's legs

Culotte — Rump (usually steak)

14

Darne	Thick slice or steak of a large fish such as salmon
Dartois	Puff-pastry rectangle stuffed with an almond-cream filling served as a dessert. Or with meat or fish and served as an hors d'oeuvre
Datte	Date
Daube	Meat (various types) stewed in red wine with onions, bacon and mushrooms
Daube	Beef with tomatoes, olives, onions and mushrooms
Dauphinoise	With Dauphine potatoes
Daurade	Gilt-headed sea bream
Dinde	Turkey
Dindonneau	Young turkey
Diplomate	Sponge pudding, generally with chocolate and strawberries in layers, covered with cream or custard
Dorade	Red sea bream
Du Barry, à la	Garnished with cauliflower, with or without cheese sauce
Duchesse, Pommes	Potatoes puréed with egg yolk

Échalote	Shallot
Échine	Loin of pork
Éclair	Long choux pastry with cream or custard filling, topped with chocolate, coffee or vanilla icing
Écrevisse	Freshwater crayfish
Émincé	Sliver or thin slice. Term used for various dishes featuring thin-sliced meat
Encornet	Squid
Endive	Chicory, usually served raw in salads, or braised with ham and a cheese sauce as a main dish
Entrecôte	Rib or sirloin steak
Entremets	Dessert or sweet course
Épaule	Shoulder of mutton, lamb, pork or veal
Épice	Spice
Épi de maïs	Sweetcorn
Épinards	Spinach
Escalope	Slice of meat, especially veal, lightly fried in butter. ~ **cordon bleu** - filled with ham and cheese
Escargot	Snail
Espadon	Swordfish
Estouffade	Meat stew with wine and vegetables
Estouffade de haricots blancs	Stew of white haricot beans with pork, tomatoes and garlic
Estragon	Tarragon
Esturgeon	Sturgeon
Étouffée, à l'	Method of cooking food slowly in a tightly covered pan with little liquid
Étuvée, à l'	Stewed, braised
Éventail, en	Fan-shaped

Fagots	Meat balls made with liver and fat, speciality of Charentes
Faisan	Pheasant
Far Breton	A batter pudding from Brittany, usually with raisins and prunes
Farce	Stuffing
Farci(e)	Stuffed
Faux-filet	Sirloin steak (also called contre-filet)
Fenouil	Fennel
Feuillantine	Puff pastry
Feuille de vigne	Vine leaf
Feuilleté	Flaky pastry with sweet or savoury filling
Feuilletée, pâte	Light flaky pastry
Fève	Broad bean. Also the name given to the little figure hidden in the **Galette des Rois**
Ficelle picarde	Pancake filled with ham and mushrooms, and a béchamel sauce
Figue	Fig. ~ **de Barbarie** - prickly pear
Filet	Fillet. A tender, boneless cut of meat which can be divided into five different cuts: beefsteak (the least tender), chateaubriand, fillet steak, tournedos and filet mignon (the most tender)
Fine de claire	Type of cultivated oyster (see **Huître**)
Fines herbes (or **Ciboulette**)	Chives
Flageolet	Kidney bean
Flamande, à la	In the Flemish style: meat served with bacon, carrots, cabbage, potatoes and turnips

Flambé(e)	Flamed in brandy or other spirit
Flamiche	Leek (sometimes pumpkin) and cheese tart. Or **flamique**: similar to a **quiche** but covered with a thin layer of pastry
Flammekueche	Onion, cream, bacon and cream cheese flan. Also called **tarte flambée**
Flan	Open pastry tart. Also a name for **crème caramel**
Flétan	Halibut
Florentine	With spinach
Foie	Liver
Foie gras	Goose or duck liver, usually served in slices
Fondue	Hot sauce into which are dipped pieces of food. ~ **au fromage** - hot mixture of melted cheese and white wine into which are dipped cubes of bread on skewers
Fondue bourguignonne	Cubes of steak cooked on skewers in hot oil
Forestière, à la	Garnished with bacon and mushrooms lightly fried in butter
Four, au	Baked or roasted in an oven
Fourré(e)	Stuffed, filled with
Frais/fraîche	Fresh
Fraise	Strawberry. ~ **des bois** - wild strawberry
Framboise	Raspberry
Frangipane	Almond custard filling
Friand	Small pastry similar to a sausage roll, or a small almond cake
Fricandeau	Topside of veal. Also a dish of braised veal or a slice or fillet of fish or pork pâté cooked in a thin slice of pork or a sausage-meat ball
Fricassée	Stew of white meat or poultry

18

	served in a creamy white sauce, sometimes including mushrooms and onions
Frisée	Curly endive
Frites	Chips
Friture	Mixture of small fried fish
Fromage	Cheese
Fromage blanc	Mild, soft, slightly salty cheese with the consistency of yogurt
Fromage de tête	Brawn
Fruit de la passion	Passion fruit
Fruits confits	Candied fruit
Fruits de mer	Seafood in general, especially refers to shell-fish
Fumé(e)	Smoked or cured

G

Galantine	Cooked meat, fish or vegetables in jelly, served cold
Galette	Pastry, pancake or cake
Galette des Rois	A flaky galette served on Epiphany
Galette de blé noir	Buck-wheat flour pancake usually filled with cheese, meat or fish
Galette de pommes de terre	Potato cake
Gamba	Large prawn
Ganache	Chocolate and crème fraîche mixture used to fill cakes
Garbure	Thick vegetable soup (cabbage, peas, haricot beans and garlic) with pork, sausage or **confit**
Gardon	Roach
Garni(e)	With vegetables
Gâteau	Cake. ~ **basque** - pastry filled with custard or fruit (cherries or plums); ~ **battu** - type of brioche, from Picardie; ~ **breton** - large, plain but rich cake; ~ **manqué** - sponge-cake topped with praline and crystallized fruit; ~ **de riz** - rice pudding; ~ **de Savoie** - light sponge cake
Gaufre	Waffle. ~ **fourrée** - waffle with filling
Gaufrette	Wafer biscuit
Gazpacho	A cold, highly-flavoured soup
Gelée	Aspic, jelly
Génoise	Rich sponge cake used as a basis for a wide variety of desserts
Gésier	Gizzard
Gibelotte	Stew of hare or rabbit, like a fricassée
Gibier	Game. ~ **d'eau** - waterfowl

20

Gigot de	Leg of (usually lamb or mutton)
Gigue	Haunch (of venison or wild boar)
Gingembre	Ginger
Girolle	Apricot-coloured fungi, mushroom
Gîte	Leg of beef
Givré(e)	Frosted. Also, frosted citrus-fruit **sorbets** served in their skins
Glacé(e)	Iced, crystallized, glazed
Glace	Ice cream
Gnocchi	Dumplings of semolina, potato or choux paste
Gougère	Round-shaped, egg and Gruyère cheese choux pastry
Goujon	Gudgeon fish
Goulasch	Goulash. Beef stew with diced onions and paprika, from Hungary
Gourmandises	Delicacies, sweetmeats
Goyave	Guava
Gratin	Dish of which the topping, usually of cheese, is browned in the oven to form a crust. ~ **dauphinois** - layers of thinly sliced potatoes baked in milk, with grated cheese and nutmeg; ~ **savoyard** - thinly sliced potatoes baked with cheese and butter. **Au** ~ - in the form of a *gratin*
Gratinée	Any soup that is topped with browned, grated cheese, as is the traditional French onion soup
Grecque, à la	With vegetables, mostly artichokes and mushrooms, stewed with oil and herbs and served cold
Grenade	Pomegranate
Grenouille	Frog. **Cuisses de** ~ - frogs' legs
Gribiche	Mayonnaise with gherkins, capers, egg yolks and herbs
Grillade	Grilled meat

Griotte (or **Griottine**)	Morello cherry
Grondin	Gurnard (used in bouillabaisse)
Groseille	Currant. ~ **noire** - blackcurrant; ~ **rouge** - redcurrant; ~ **à maquereau** - gooseberry

Haché(e)	Minced
Hachis	Minced or chopped up; ~ **parmentier** - shepherd's pie
Hareng	Herring. ~ **à l'huile** - herring cured in oil; ~ **fumé** - kippered herring; ~ **saur** - smoked herring
Haricot	Bean, including true beans (i.e. kidney beans) and edible bean pods (i.e. French beans). ~ **blanc** - white bean, either fresh **(frais)** or dried **(sec)**; ~ **rouge** - red kidney bean; ~ **vert** - French bean or string bean
Harissa	A spiced paste made with pimento, cayenne pepper, oil, garlic and coriander. Used mainly with couscous
Hochepot	Thick meat and vegetable stew from Flanders, made with oxtail, beef, mutton and cuts of pork. The vegetables include: cabbage, leeks, potatoes, etc.
Homard	Lobster. ~ **à l'armoricaine** - lobster sautéed in oil, flambéed in cognac and served in a cream and wine sauce with onions, garlic, tomatoes and herbs. Also called **homard à l'américaine.** ~ **thermidor** - sautéed lobster served in the shell in a creamy white wine sauce topped with parmesan cheese and browned
Hors-d'œuvre	First course or starter
Huile	Oil
Huître	Oyster

I and I

Île flottante	Dessert of whipped poached egg-whites floating in vanilla custard and sometimes sprinkled with chopped almonds
Impératrice, à l'	Desserts with candied fruits soaked in kirsch. Also a base for desserts composed of rice, cream, custard and crystallized fruit
Indienne, à l'	Indian style: with curry sauce and rice
Jambon	Ham. ~ **blanc** - Cooking ham or boiling ham. Also called *jambon de Paris.* ~ **de Bayonne** - delicately cured ham eaten raw; ~ **cru** - uncooked ham; raw ham; ~ **de campagne** or ~ **de montagne** or ~ **de pays** - country ham smoked and salted according to local custom; ~ **fumé** - smoked ham; ~ **de Parme** - Parma ham. Smoked ham eaten raw; ~ **de York** - ready-cooked ham
Jambonneau	Knuckle of pork
Jardin, du	From the garden (i.e. fresh)
Jardinière, à la	With diced mixed fresh vegetables
Jarret de veau	Stew of shin of veal
Julienne	Thinly-cut vegetables used in garnishes or sauces
Julienne, consommé	Clear soup garnished with thin strips of carrots, leeks, celery and cabbage
Jus, au	Served in the juice from the roast meat

K and L

Kouign amann	Type of Breton puff-pastry cake layered with sugar
Kumquat	Kumquat. Variety of tiny orange
Laitue	Lettuce
Laitue romaine	Cos lettuce
Lamelle	Thin slice, flake
Langouste	Spiny lobster, crayfish or crawfish
Langoustine	Scampi, pink shellfish, Dublin Bay prawn
Langue, de bœuf or **de veau**	(Ox or veal) tongue
Langue de chat	Small, thin, oval-shaped, crispy biscuit often served with iced desserts and also used to make puddings
Lapereau	Young rabbit
Lapin	Rabbit. ~ **à la flamande** - rabbit cooked Flanders-style, marinated in red wine, braised with prunes and olives
Lard	Bacon
Lard de poitrine	Fat belly of pork
Lardé(e)	Larded, referring to meat which has been wrapped or picked with lard prior to cooking
Lardons	Strips of bacon or diced, fried pieces of bacon. Used as an ingredient in hotpots or as a garnish
Laurier	Bay (herb)
Légumes	Vegetables
Lentilles	Lentils
Letchi	Lychee
Lieu	Cod-like fish
Lièvre	Hare. **Civet de** ~ - Jugged hare
Limande	Flatfish similar to sole

Lit, sur un	On a bed of one or more ingredients used as a base on which others are served
Lotte (de mer)	Monkfish, anglerfish
Loup de mer	Bass

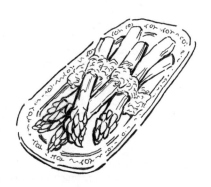

M

Macaron	Macaroon, almond cake
Macédoine de fruits or ~ **de légumes**	Mixed, diced fruit or vegetables
Mâche	Lamb's lettuce. Small, dark, green leaf
Macreuse	Cut of beef shoulder
Madeleine	Small, fluted sponge cake
Magret (de canard)	Boned breast (of duck) grilled or fried. Can now also refer to other poultry
Maïs	Maize. Corn. Sweetcorn. **Épi de** ~ - corn on the cob
Maison, de la	Of the restaurant, house speciality
Mandarine	Tangerine
Mange-tout	'Eat-all': edible peas and pods. Sugar peas
Mangue	Mango
Maquereau	Mackerel
Marcassin	Young wild boar
Marée	Fresh seafood
Marengo, poulet (or **veau**)	Sautéed chicken (or veal) cooked with onions, tomatoes, mushrooms, olive oil, white wine, garlic, herbs
Marennes (blanche)	Flat-shelled oyster
Mariné(e)	Marinated or pickled
Marmite	(Cooking) pot. ~ **dieppoise** - fish stew
Marquise au chocolat	Rich chocolate sponge cake with cream
Marron	Chestnut
Marron glacé	Crystallized, candied sweet chestnut
Matelote	General name for a stew of fresh-water fish cooked in wine, e.g. ~ **d'anguilles**

Méchoui	Lamb or sheep roasted over coals and constantly basted. Also, a barbecue where the meat is cooked.
Médaillon (de)	Round piece of meat. Also called **tournedos** (beef or veal), and **noisette** (lamb)
Melba	Served with ice cream and raspberry sauce
Méli-mélo	Hotch-potch, mixture
Melon surprise	Chilled melon filled with fruit and sprinkled with liqueur
Mendiants	See **Quatre mendiants**
Menthe	Mint
Merguez	Spicy grilled sausage from North Africa
Meringue glacée	Meringue with ice cream
Merlan	Whiting, hake
Mérou	Grouper-like fish used in bouillabaisse
Merlu	Hake
Meunière, sole	Sole cooked in butter with lemon juice and parsley
Miel	Honey
Mignon	A small, tender fillet steak, like a *filet mignon*
Millefeuille	Puff pastry with numerous thin layers filled with crème pâtissière and jam or cream, or filled with fish, or vegetables and a cream sauce
Mimosa	With chopped hardboiled egg-yolks
Mirabelle	A small, yellow plum
Miroton de boeuf	Beef sliced and boiled in an onion sauce
Mode, à la	In the manner/style of
Moelle	Beef marrow. **Os à ~** - bone-marrow
Moka	Coffee-flavoured
Montagne, de	From the mountains as in **jambon de montagne**

Mont-blanc	A cream and chestnut dessert topped with whipped cream
Morceau	Piece, morsel
Morille	Highly flavoured, dark brown, mushroom. Morel
Mortadelle	Italian mortadella sausage served as an hors d'œuvre
Morue	Cod. ~ **salée** - salt cod. ~ **fraîche** - fresh cod
Mouclade	Mussels cooked with turmeric in a creamy white wine sauce
Moules	Mussels. ~ **à la mariniere** - cooked in white wine, onion and parsley sauce and shallots; ~ **farcies** - filled with a butter, parsley and garlic sauce then covered with breadcrumbs and grilled
Mousse	A dessert made with whipped egg-white or cream. ~ **au chocolat** - chocolate mousse. Also a light savoury dish from whipped ingredients
Mousseline	Generic name for mousse dishes containing whipped cream and/or egg-whites, such as purées of fish. **Gâteau** ~ - mixture used for light, cakes and pastries
Moutarde	Mustard
Mouton	Mutton
Mulet	Grey mullet
Mûre	Blackberry, mulberry
Muscade	Nutmeg
Museau de porc or **de bœuf**	Sliced muzzle of pork (or beef) served with shallots and parsley in vinaigrette
Myrtille	Bilberry, blueberry
Mystère	A meringue desert with ice cream and chocolate. Also, ice cream with a macaroon centre

Napolitain	Large layered cake composed of almond pastry with various fruit jams
Napolitaine, tranche	Ice cream dessert comprising layers of ice cream and iced mousse; brick-shaped and cut into slices
Nappé(e)	Covered with a sauce
Nature (or **au naturel**)	Plain, ungarnished
Navarin	Stew of mutton or lamb, cooked with onions and potatoes. ~ **printanier** - with spring vegetables
Navet	Turnip
Nègre en chemise	Chocolate ice cream covered with whipped cream
Neige, à la	See **Oeuf**
Nid	Nest
Noisette	Hazelnut
Noisette (d'agneau, etc.)	Small, round piece of meat, usually lamb or mutton, cut from the fillet or rib or top leg
Noisettine	Small, short pastry cake with hazelnut cream filling
Noix	Walnut. ~ **de cajou** - cashew nut; ~ **de coco** - coconut
Noix (de veau)	Topside of leg (veal)
Nonnette	Iced gingerbread cake
Normande, à la	Normandy-style: with cream, apples, Calvados or cider
Nougat glacé	Chilled nougat-based dessert
Nougatine	Small, layered sponge cake with praline cream and often a chocolate icing
Nouille	Noodle

Oeuf de Pâques	Easter egg
Oeufs	Eggs. ~ **brouillés** - scrambled; ~ **en cocotte** - cooked in a ramekin with cream; ~ **à la coque** or **mollet** - soft-boiled; ~ **durs** - hard-boiled; ~ **en meurette** - poached in a white wine sauce; ~ **à la poêle** or **sur le plat** - fried
Oeufs à la Florentine	Boiled eggs topped with spinach which is then covered with a **Mornay sauce**
Oeufs à la neige	Poached egg-whites in vanilla custard. Also called **île flottante**
Oignon	Onion
Oie	Goose
Omelette au choix	Omelette with choice of filling or ~ **nature** - plain omelette
Omelette Norvégienne or **Omelette surprise**	Baked Alaska. Sponge base topped with ice cream, covered with meringue and baked
Onglet	Flank of beef
Orange givrée	Orange sorbet served in a hollowed-out orange, often served straight from the freezer
Os	Bone. **À l'** ~ - on the bone
Oseille	Sorrel
Osso bucco	Veal braised in white wine, tomatoes, onions and garlic
Oursin	Sea urchin. Its flesh is eaten either raw or mixed with scrambled eggs or soups

Paëlla	Spanish rice dish with mixed seafood, poultry and vegetables
Pain	Bread. ~ **de seigle** - rye bread; ~ **d'épice** - gingerbread; **petit** ~ - bread roll. Or a loaf (fish, meat etc.) ~ **de poisson** - fish loaf; ~ **de viande** - meat loaf
Palette de porc	Shoulder of pork
Palmier	Palm-shaped sweet puff pastry
Palourde	Clam. ~ **farcie** - stuffed with shallots, cream and cheese; speciality of Brittany
Pamplemousse	Grapefruit
Panaché(e)	Mixed
Panais	Parsnip
Pané(e)	Breadcrumbed
Pannequet	A type of savoury pancake, folded into four, topped with sugar, cheese, etc. and browned
Papaye	Pawpaw fruit, papaya
Papillote, en	Cooked in oiled paper (or foil)
Paquets, en	In parcels
Parfait	An iced mousse, ice cream
Parfum	Flavour or aroma (usually of ice creams or sorbets)
Paris-Brest	Ring-shaped cake made of choux pastry, filled with praline butter cream, and topped with chopped almonds
Parmentier	In general, garnished, filled or made with potatoes, as in **hachis Parmentier**
Pastèque	Watermelon
Patate douce	Sweet potato or yam
Pâté en croûte	A preparation of meat, game, fowl or fish baked in a pastry case and served cold or hot

Pâté en terrine	A rich mixture of meat, game, fowl or fish baked in a pottery dish called **a terrine**
Pâte d'amande	Almond paste, marzipan
Pâtes (fraîches)	(Fresh) pasta; noodles
Pâtisserie	General term for pastries and cakes (also the shop where they are sold)
Paupiettes	Thin slices of meat, or fish, wrapped round a savoury filling, like a beef olive, then gently braised
Pavé	('Paving-stone') Thick slice of meat, such as beefsteak
Pays, de	From the region
Paysanne, à la	Country-style: meat served with carrots, turnips, onions, celery, potatoes and sometimes bacon
Pêches melba	Poached peaches or peaches in syrup with vanilla ice cream and raspberry sauce
Perdreau	Young partridge
Perdrix	Partridge
Périgourdine, à la	With truffles and sometimes also foie gras
Persillade	Mixture of chopped parsley and garlic
Pesto	A sauce made from olive oil and basil
Petits-fours	Small biscuits, chocolates, cakes, candied fruit served after the meal usually with coffee
Petits pois	Peas
Petit salé	Salt pork
Pied de porc	Pig's trotter
Pigeonneau	Young pigeon
Pignon	Pine nut, pine kernel
Pilaf (or pilau)	Savoury rice dish mixed with other ingredients such as white meat and/or shellfish

Pilon	Drumstick (poultry)
Piment	Red pepper or pimento. Also refers to hot spices: cayenne pepper, chilli powder, paprika, etc.
Piment doux	Sweet pepper, also called **poivron**
Pintade	Guinea-fowl
Pintadeau	Young guinea-fowl
Piperade	Basque country omelette or scrambled eggs with tomatoes, peppers, onions, garlic and, sometimes, Bayonne ham
Pissaladière	Open pie which is topped with puréed onions, anchovies or sardines, black olives, and sometimes tomatoes
Pissenlit	Dandelion. The leaf can be served as a salad with cubes of fried bacon and fried bread
Pistache	Green pistachio nut
Pistou	Similar to the Italian pesto. Sauce of basil, garlic and olive oil made into a paste
Pithiviers	Puff pastry and almond gâteau filled with cream
Plat	Dish. Also a course on the menu
Plat du jour	Dish of the day; today's special
Plateau de fruits de mer	Large plate of various shellfish (usually including mussels, prawns, winkles and cockles)
Plateau de fromages	Cheese board
Plie	Plaice
Plombières	Sweet with vanilla ice cream, kirsch, candied fruit and crème Chantilly
Poché(e)	Poached
Pointe (d'asperge)	(Asparagus) tip
Poire Belle-Hélène	Poached pear, served with vanilla ice-cream and topped with a hot chocolate sauce

Poire vigneronne or **poire au vin rouge**	Pear in red wine
Poireau	Leek
Pois	Peas
Pois cassés	Split peas
Pois chiches	Chickpeas
Poisson	Fish
Poisson d'eau douce	Freshwater fish
Poisson fumé	Smoked fish
Poitrine	Breast cut of veal, pork, lamb or mutton
Poivrade	A peppery sauce with wine vinegar, cooked vegetables
Poivre	Pepper
Poivron	Capsicum, sweet red or green pepper
Polenta	Maize or corn-meal porridge which, when set is fried in butter until golden brown. Can also be topped with cheese
Pomme	Apple. ~ **bonne femme** - baked apples
Pommes de terre	Potatoes. ~ **allumettes** - thin and fried; ~ **à l'anglaise** - boiled potatoes; ~ **boulangère** - sliced potatoes cooked with onions; ~ **dauphine** - deep-fried croquettes of puréed potatoes mixed with choux paste; ~ **duchesse** - smooth blend of potatoes, eggs and butter, piped around a dish and baked, ~ **frites** - fried chips; ~ **gratinées** - browned with cheese; ~ **lyonnaises** - sliced and sautéed with onions; ~ **mousseline** - puréed potatoes mixed with butter, egg-yolks and whipped cream; ~ **noisettes** - small potatoes fried in butter; ~ **en robe de chambre** or **en robe des**

	champs - jacket potatoes; ~ **vapeur** - boiled
Porc	Pork, porkmeat or pig. **Carré de porc** - loin roast; **côte de porc** - pork chop; **filet de porc** - fillet or tenderloin; **poitrine de porc** - bacon or belly
Porcelet	Suckling pig
Potage	Thick soup
Potage bonne femme	Potato and leek soup
Pot-au-feu	Meat and vegetables cooked in a stock
Pot-pourri	A selection
Potée	Thick soup of cabbage, beans, etc.
Potiron	Pumpkin, also called **citrouille** and **courge**
Potje vleesch	Northern terrine of mixed meats (rabbit, pork, veal)
Poularde (demi-deuil)	Large hen (studded with truffles and poached)
Poule	Hen
Poule au pot	Chicken boiled in a stock. ~ **d'Henri IV** - chicken stuffed with ham and liver and cooked in wine
Poulet	Chicken. ~ **à la broche** - spit-roasted chicken; ~ **basquaise** - chicken with tomatoes and peppers; ~ **de Bresse** - free range, corn-fed chicken from the Bresse region
Poulpe	Octopus
Poussin	Small baby chicken
Praire	Small clam
Pralin	Mixture of crushed nuts and caramel used as a filling or a topping
Praline	Caramel-coated almond
Pré-salé	Salt-meadow or salt-marsh. **Agneau de pré-salé** - lamb raised on salt

	marshes
Primeur	Describes fruit and vegetables that are the first of the season
Printanière, à la	('Spring-style') With early spring vegetables such as carrots, turnips, peas and beans
Profiterole	Choux pastry puff, filled with sweet custard pastry-cream **(crème pâtissière)**, or whipped cream, or with savoury purées or cheese
Provençale, à la	Provençal-style: cooked and served with tomatoes, garlic, olive oil, etc.
Prune	Plum
Pruneau	Prune
Puits d'amour	('Well of love') Flaky-pastry crown filled with pastry-cream **(crème pâtissière)** or thick gooseberry jelly
Purée (de pommes de terre)	Mashed (potatoes)

Quatre mendiants	Dessert of figs, almonds, hazelnuts and raisins
Quasi (de veau)	Thick part of loin of veal (chump)
Quenelle	Poached mousse or light dumpling of fish or poultry. ~ **de brochet** - small pike dumpling, steamed and served in a cream sauce
Quetsche	Small, purple plum
Queue de boeuf	Oxtail
Queue d'écrevisse, gratin de	Crayfish tail (in a creamy sauce and served as a gratin)
Quiche	Open pastry tart filled with a variety of savoury ingredients: bacon, ham, cheese, etc. ~ **lorraine** - quiche filled with smoked bacon, eggs, cream and cheese

Râble de lièvre or **de lapin**	Saddle of hare or of rabbit
Raclette	Cheese fondue from Savoy eaten hot with pieces of baked potato
Radis	Radish
Ragoût	Meat, fowl or fish stew cooked slowly in a stock, with or without vegetables
Raie	Skate
Raifort	Horseradish
Raisin	Grape. ~ **de Corinthe** - currant; ~ **de Smyrne** - sultana; ~ **sec** - raisin
Râpé(e)	Grated or shredded
Rascasse	Scorpion fish
Ratatouille	Provençal dish made with aubergines, onions, courgettes, garlic, red peppers and tomatoes in olive oil, served either hot or cold
Raviole	Savoury pastry filling with goat's cheese
Ravioli	Small squares of pasta filled with meat
Réglisse	Liquorice
Reine, à la	With chicken or puréed chicken, and cream
Reine-Claude	Greengage
Religieuse	Individual pastry cake made with a large profiterole topped by a small one, both filled with coffee or chocolate cream
Rémoulade	Mayonnaise made with mustard, capers and herbs
Rhubarbe	Rhubarb
Rillettes de porc or **d'oie**	Potted pork or goose
Ris d'agneau or **de veau**	Lamb or calf sweetbreads

Risotto	Rice cooked with a meat stock and mixed with meat,mushrooms, onions, cheese, shellfish…
Rissole	A deep-fried puff-pastry roll filled with minced meat
Riz	Rice. ~ **au lait** - sweet rice pudding; ~ **à l'impératrice** - cold rice pudding with candied fruits
Rognon	Kidney, normally lamb's or calf's
Romaine, laitue	Cos lettuce
Romarin	Rosemary
Romstek	Rump steak
Rondelle	Slice, ring
Roquette	Salad green
Rosbif	Roast beef
Rosette	Sliced, large dry pork sausage from Lyon
Rossini	With foie gras and truffles
Rôti	Roast. A meat-roast; ~ **à la broche** - spit roast
Rouelle (de veau)	Round piece or slice of veal
Rouget	Red mullet
Rouille	Orange-coloured sauce with peppers, garlic and saffron
Roulade (de)	Rolled piece of meat or fish usually stuffed (with)
Roussette	Rock salmon. Dog fish
Roux	Flour and butter base for sauces
Rutabaga	Swede

Sabayon	Zabaglione. Egg yolks whipped with wine and served as a light mousse or eaten on its own as a dessert
Sablé	A crumbly shortbread biscuit
Safran	Saffron
Saint-Honoré	Round choux pastry cake, iced with sugar and filled with cream
Saint-Jacques	**Noix (de coquille) Saint-Jacques** - white flesh of the scallop. See also **Coquilles**
St-Pierre	John Dory
Saison, de	When in season
Salade	Salad. Lettuce. ~ **niçoise** - tomatoes, beans, potatoes, black olives, anchovy, lettuce, olive oil, perhaps tuna; ~ **composée** - mixed salad; ~ **panachée** - mixed salad; ~ **verte** - green salad; ~ **waldorf** - salad with apples, walnuts, celeriac
Salami	An Italian pork sausage
Salé, petit	Pickled pork or ham
Salmis	A game-fowl dish in which the bird is simmered in red wine sauce
Salsifis	Salsify (vegetable)
Sandre	Pikeperch, zander
Sanglier	Wild boar
Sarments	Wine twigs, used for grilling steak in Bordeaux
Sarrasin	Buckwheat
Sarriette	Savory, bitter herb
Sauce	Sauce. ~ **Béarnaise** - rich, creamy sauce made with egg yolks, shallots, butter, white wine and tarragon vinegar; ~ **Diane** - peppered

41

cream sauce for beef or game; ~ **Hollandaise** - sauce with butter, egg yolk and lemon juice, served with eggs, fish. ~ **Madère** - stock (demi-glace) mixed with Madeira wine; ~ **Mornay** - béchamel sauce with grated cheese; ~ **Nantua** - white sauce with cream, puréed crayfish and butter; ~ **piquante** - brown spicy sauce with vinegar, shallots, capers, gherkins, herbs and spices; ~ **ravigote** - thick vinaigrette mixed with chopped gherkins, capers, tarragon, chervil and other herbs; ~ **Soubise** cream sauce with onions; ~ **suprême** - creamy white sauce; ~ **tartare** - a mayonnaise sauce with onions, capers and herbs

Saucisse	Freshly-made sausage, which must be cooked before eating; ~ **de Strasbourg** - frankfurter sausage, of smoked port and beef; ~ **de Toulouse** - large (usually grilled) sausage
Saucisson (à l'ail)	(Garlic) sausage. ~ **sec** - dry sausage
Sauge	Sage
Saumon	Salmon. ~ **fumé** - smoked salmon
Saumonette	Sea eel, dogfish
Sauté(e)	Shallow fried
Savarin	See **Baba au rhum**
Savoyarde	With (Gruyère) cheese and potatoes

Scarole	Endive (chicory)
Seiche	Squid or cuttlefish
Sel marin, sel de mer	Sea salt
Selle	Saddle
Selon grosseur	Priced according to size and/or weight
Semoule	Semolina
Semoule de couscous	Couscous
Serpolet	Wild thyme
Sirop	Syrup
Soja, pousse de	Soya bean (soy beansprout). **Sauce de** ~ - soy sauce; **viande de** ~ - meat substitute
Sole (limande)	(Lemon) sole. ~ **à la Dieppoise** - sole fillets with mussels, shrimps, wine and cream
Sorbet	Water ice in various fruit flavours
Soubise	Purée of onions and rice. **Sauce** ~ - white, onion sauce
Soufflé	Sweet or savoury dishes made of egg-yolks and beaten egg whites and baked
Soupe	Soup. ~ **à l'oignon** - onion soup
Souris d'agneau	Knuckle of lamb
Steak tartare	Raw minced steak
Strasbourgeoise, à la	Strasbourg style: foie gras, sauerkraut, bacon
Strudel	Pastry filled with apples, currants and cinnamon
Sucré(e)	Sweetened
Suprême (de volaille)	Boneless breast of poultry. Also describes a fish fillet

Taboulé	Crushed wheat, parsley, mint with onions, tomatoes and lemon juice
Tapenade	Purée of tuna, capers olives and anchovies. Usually spread on toast
Tartare	See **Steak tartare** or **Sauce tartare**
Tarte	Open flan. ~ **Tatin** - upside down tart with caramelised apples; ~ **flambée** - see **Flammekueche**
Tartelette	Small, open tart with either a sweet or a savoury filling
Tartine	Slice of bread, usually served with a topping
Terrine	Coarse pâté. ~ **de foie de volaille** - liver pâté
Tête de nègre	Round meringue covered with chocolate
Tête de veau vinaigrette	Calf's head vinaigrette
Tête, fromage de	Brawn
Thermidor	See **Homard**
Thon	Tuna
Thym	Thyme
Tian	Preparations, such as the mixed vegetable **gratins** of Provence, cooked in a **tian**: a shallow, earthenware, cooking dish
Timbale	Mould in which the contents are steamed. Also, small fish or vegetable mousse or jelly served as an hors d'oeuvre or garnish
Tomate	Tomato. ~ **farcie** - stuffed tomato
Topinambour	Jerusalem artichoke
Torte	Sweet-filled flan. Or rich cakes, usually with cream
Tournedos	Small, round fillet steaks of beef

	~ **chasseur** - with shallots, mushrooms, tomatoes; ~ **rossini** - with goose liver, truffles, port and croûtons; ~ **cordon rouge** - steak with ham and foie gras, served in a cognac sauce
Touron	A cake, pastry or loaf made from almond paste and filled with candied fruits and pistachio nuts. From the Languedoc region
Tourte	Covered savoury or sweet tart or pie
Tourteau	Large crab
Tourteau fromager	Goat's cheese gâteau, from Poitou
Tranche	Slice
Tranche napolitaine	Mixed flavour ice-cream
Travers de porc	Spare rib of pork
Tripes	Tripe. ~ **à la mode de Caen** - tripe cooked slowly in cider and Calvados with trotters, onions, carrots and herbs
Trompettes de la mort	Edible fungi, also called **corne d'abondance**
Trou normand	Calvados or Calvados flavoured sorbet enjoyed between courses
Truffe	Truffle. Black, exotic, tuber
Truffe	Chocolate sweet with a dark, buttery centre
Truffé(e)	With truffles
Truite	Trout. ~ **au bleu** - trout poached in water and vinegar; ~ **arc-en-ciel** - rainbow trout; ~ **saumonée** - salmon trout; ~ **meunière** - dipped in flour and sautéed in butter, with parsley and lemon
Tuiles	Small almond biscuits
Turbot (or **turbotin**)	Turbot

45

𝒱 to 𝒵

Vacherin Dessert of tiered meringue rings filled with whipped cream or ice-cream, and served with strawberries

Vanille Vanilla

Vapeur, à la Steamed, boiled. **Pommes (de terre)** ~ - boiled, steamed potatoes

Varié(e) Assorted, mixed, as in hors d'oeuvres variés

Veau Veal. **Escalope de ~ à la Viennoise** - slice of veal coated with egg and breadcrumbs and fried; **escalope de ~ Milanaise** - with macaroni, tomatoes, ham, mushrooms; **escalope de ~ pané** - thin slice in flour, eggs and bread crumbs; **tête de ~** - calf's head

Velouté White sauce made from veal or chicken stock thickened with flour and butter

Velouté de volaille Thick chicken soup

Venaison Venison

Vermicelle Vermicelli

Viande Meat in general. ~ **de cheval** - horsemeat

Vichy With carrots

Vichyssoise Creamy potato and leek soup, served cold

Viennoise Food (usually veal) coated with egg and breadcrumbs and fried

Vinaigre Vinegar

Vinaigrette French dressing with wine vinegar, oil, etc.

Vive Weever fish

Vol-au-vent	Puff pastry case filled with various fillings
Volaille	Poultry and fowl
Waterzooi (or **Waterzoi**)	Freshwater fish or chicken stewed with vegetables in a creamy sauce
Yaourt	Yogurt
Zucchini	Courgettes, baby marrows

MAKE THE MOST OF YOUR FRENCH AND GET MORE OUT OF FRANCE...

...with our unique range of products and services for learners of French.

At Concorde Publications we aim to help you enjoy your French – whatever the stage you are at – and improve it at the same time. With our unique range of products and services you can develop your grasp of spoken French, read articles and stories in French, meet people who share your interest in the language (including in France) and much more.

Long-established publishers of books and magazines, we have a reputation for quality and for innovative support for learners of French. This booklet is just one small example of the assistance we provide. This assistance also extends to organising holidays in France that combine language learning and visits to some of the country's loveliest locations.

To find out more about all that we do, please visit our website or contact us directly.

Concorde French Language Publications

Telephone (U.K.): 01622 749167
Telephone (International): + 44 1622 749167
www.concordefrench.com